A JOURNEY OF THE HEART

A small book of poems dedicated to children fighting MD

Helena L. MacCallum Schnieders

RiverRock, Inc., Publishing Division
St. Charles and St. Louis, Missouri

i

A JOURNEY OF THE HEART
A small book of poems dedicated to children fighting MD
By Helena L. MacCallum Schnieders

Published by RiverRock, Inc.
St. Charles and St. Louis, Missouri
P.O. Box 210205
St. Louis, Missouri (MO) 63121
Phone: (314) 610-9999

First Printing, 2000

Printed in the United States of America.

Library of Congress Catalog Card Number: 00 091700
ISBN: 0-9700728-0-5

This Book is dedicated to
My son - my inspiration & my life
Andrew Jerome Schnieders

All royalties will be donated to the
Muscular Dystrophy Association and
the Duchenne Parent Project for
Muscular Dystrophy Research

Section I

A Parent's Heart

My Andrew

I could only give you
A box of sunshine
Wrapped with ribbons of love.
A box of dreams, never
Promises too easily broken.
I could only sing you
A lullaby and wake you with a smile.
The riches of kings
Were beyond my reach,
Only time and patience on my side.
Story books and balloons took
Us 'round the world
Where you slew dragons for me.
My knight has grown into a man
With other worlds to conquer,
While I still sail
Into tomorrow with only
A box of sunshine
Wrapped with ribbons of love.

At the Piano

She who wishes
  To see the gates of
Heaven open, has only
  To listen to music
Played by her child.
  This, not all the angels
On harps can match in
  The heart of a mother.

Thought

My child has grown so much in size
And now the wonder and merriment are
Replaced in his eyes by wisdom
and seeking for a time yet unknown
That will find him a father
With a child of his own.

Red River Gorge

One hundred yellow butterflies
Danced through shafts of
Sunlight while the
Silence of the woods
Was broken only by the rush
Of a waterfall and the
Laughter of a child, on the
Threshold of manhood,
Rediscovering the treasures
Which a mountain stream
Has to offer, that only
A boy can find.
These are gifts to a mother's
Memory, that money can't buy,
And not even time
Can take away.

Honor Band

I hear the music within my heart,
Dancing on butterfly wings,
Shimmering in moonlight reflected
On water's edge, moving, gliding,
Marching to the drummer's delight.
My soul soars and glides with
Syncopation through the winter air,
Growing, swelling, bursting with pride
As music's children weave their spell.

Ode to a Whisker

I watch my cats with great delight
As tails swish from left to right
Their faces are so full of mirth
The gray one, why she wears a smirk,
They romp, they jump, they run and play
With you my house is full today
And when their play is set and done
They lie to nap in the noonday sun.

His Proper Name is Andrew

You say hello
Like Tigger
And look a little
Like Pooh
But I am only
Alice
Looking through
The glass
As you!

Parenting

Children are conceived in our passion
And born from our dreams.
We plan and conspire to greatness
Only to find time has passed
Leaving us with these
Mirror-like images full-grown
Before our eyes. We mold and
Pray and then one day
Awake to find we're
Riding on the coattails of
Their dreams and we burst
Forth in pride with a parent's
Primal scream, "That's My Boy!"

The Note

The note said,
"I am learning
to write on a
computer. I like
you. I think
you are sweet.
Love your student,
Shelia." I put
It on the
Refrigerator to remind
Me why I teach.
Thank you Shelia,
I love you too.

Section II

A Heart In Love

1990

I welcomed the dawn of a new decade
In the arms of an Englishman,
Not a proper stuff-shirt, mind you,
But a gentle, comedic man
Who made me smile and feel special.
The sun rose gently, not red and angry,
Simply golden over a horizon of blue.
The waves calmed, a slight breeze brought
The chill and our hush was broken only by my heart.
I savored the moments for soon we would part
He to his world, and I to mine.
Years and miles held at bay two souls
United in a communion of passion.
Each time I drop a fishing line, with
No prey in sight, I will smile because
Somewhere in this world gone mad, my
Curly-headed Limey yearns to do the same.
When I chew my pen in thought,
My heart will tug, because time
Has once more robbed me of a soul mate,
As I remain destined to finish the dance alone.

Happy New Year

Hello you said
With that
Leprechaun smile and
Curly head.
I resigned to greet
The New Year on
My own, and
You with your lads
Never drink alone.
Shy, not quite,
Danced right into my heart.
Pretty girls, I'm sure
You've had your fill, and
Here I sat,
Middle-aged at that,
Thought you polite
To chat with me.
Then we left
You, Lance and I
We danced and sang
Laughed 'til dawn
To greet the sun
With a stifled yawn.
My knight rode in but,
Then you left and
Here I sit with
Just four cats and
Memories, ah,
Such memories.

Sir Lance and His Lot

his wall built,
carefully brick-by-brick
no windows, he said,
only the stairs to tomorrow
somewhere across the
open skies, and a land
too new and wide
the food so different,
people odd, but
adventure waits across
a bridge to his dream,
guitar on his knee
chums by his side
his smile and a pint
will win his way
soon he'll find,
in another day, the answer,
to the unspoken question.

Despacio Mi Amour

What have you done to me?
Again, I wait for the phone to ring.
When it does, my heart leaps.
I feel like a schoolgirl
Awaiting her first boy kiss.
Your lips are imprinted on my soul.
With each breath there is
Anticipation of a union about to be.
I cannot tell what I see in your eyes.
Though I want you, I am frightened
Of the pain that is eminent.
Passion disguised as love has
Done me in before, I must be ready.
I want a lover, not a stranger
To welcome the dawn of each
New day past the 60th year of my birth.

Found

I found you!
You are so warm and caring
You touched my heart so lightly
When you entered
I didn't know you were in.
I want to be consumed by the
Passion I feel for you.
But, you don't know you
Dwell in my heart.
I ache for you to hold me
Through the night, but I can not tell you.
I am of a time long past,
You are of the here and now.
I can only possess you in my dreams.

Hola Mi Amour

You filled me with pretty lies
Stole my heart.
Where do you put all the
Hearts you steal? Do you
Have a shelf to hold your
Collection? Do you just
Use them and cast each
Away? Is each another
Trophy for El Macho Hombre
To tell his compadres
Ah see how grand I am?
No, I'm not mad at you,
Just at myself. I'm old
Enough to know better than
To let go of my heart, but
Young enough to be
Flattered that someone still
Wanted it. Even if it was
Only for a time so brief.

Tia's Advice

My friend says
Men like intelligent
Women. I disagree.
Quoting Aristotle never
Turned a head
Quite like an undulating
Breast or a pair of
Long legs. No man
Ever whistled at a
Woman writing poetry,
Unless she had a
Pretty face framed
With thick locks of hair.

Again

Tia always gets the drummer
While I wind up with the comedian.
How interesting the rhythms of the soul
Match the unconscious desires
Manifested in our daily reality.

Questioning

They were as one,
Yet two, swimmers
Far apart on top of
The sea. Her mind
Was an untidy cupboard
Filled with little bottles.
When they were apart
She could see herself as
Half of a couple.
It was like putting
Her face against the ocean
Looking into things,
Detached, baffled, in the
Midst of a huge impenetrable silence.

Fluorescent Ripples

The water on the horizon
Was a wide satin ribbon.
A yellow moon hung like a
Golden ball in a starless sky.
Each wave broke the calm
Leaving fluorescent ripples dancing
Across the surface. My heart
Beat an uneven rhythm
Like a drummer gone mad.
You spoke words of love
Hidden beneath gentle lies.

A Sunny Saturday

I lie on the cool sand
Allowing the sun to
Soak into my skin
Re-warming the essence of
My being, once again
Wounded by misdirected
Passion. Sailboats gently
Float in and out of my
Vision. The sea
Lulls me to an inner
Peace and I
Know the healing process
Has begun.

Thought

I want to waltz under
A starry, starry sky and
Dance upon the moon.

Awaiting His Arrival

I think I have to be
In love! To experience
The pain that comes with
Passion, anticipating the
Next time I'll gaze deep within
His eyes is the
Sustenance of the soul,
As much as food is to the
Body, yes, I think
I have to be, in love to be.

El Gaupo Hombre

Words dance in my head
My heart sings a new song
Each time I hear your voice
Your kisses are more precious
Than the rarest gem the
Earth hides within her breast.
Your caresses kindle a fire
Within my soul as hot as
Mt. St. Helen erupting with all her fury.
Assure me that you are real
Not a vision from my dreams.
Encircle me with the strength of your arms
Protecting me from my fears
Away from the harsh reality that
Comes with the end of passion.

Thoughts After a Long Night

In the song they say
Love is only for the
Lucky and the strong.
Since luck is not my
Forte and strength my
Only hope, I must be
Destined to keep him, I've
Reached the conclusion I
Want a lover not a stranger
To welcome the dawn of
Each new day. A lover
Not a stranger to Fight my blues away.
Only strong arms to
Encircle me, holding me
When the night is long
A lover not a stranger
To comfort me when
Youth is gone.

The Picnic

He Said:
Traveling hopefully,
Anxious anticipation. . . suppressed by awesome scenic beauty
Breathtaking.
As first embrace, teasing.
Lips brushing, pleasing
Bouquet of good French wine,
Wholesome Irish Cheese with brown soda bread,
Hazy sunshine and Nature's ambience,
In the Ladies' View backdrop.

Fingers of summer balmy breezes, caressing
Idle chatter, closeness.
Tensions melting.

Inquisitiveness rising,
Inhibitions falling,
Fingers, touching, fondling,
Insights of amazing awareness,
Secret intimacies explored,
Sensual embraces, senses tingling
Racing imagination and reality merged.
Harmony.
ACR 1/28/99

She Said:

Halfway round the world
Caught in a dream - now reality
Anticipation heightened by the beauty unfolding outside the window
Breathtaking
Strong arms encircling trembling flesh
Lips warm, encouraging as they come together.
Heady, unsure if it is the wine or the moment
Unable to taste the morsels of cheese and bread
Only the lingering sweetness of the first wine laced kiss
The anticipated Ladies' View stretching like the word picture
Beyond imagination, now
Real.

Nervous chatter, masking the tension
Melting under his gaze
Surrounded by sweet breezes.
Will I awake to find it is only, once again a dream?

Curiosity conquering inhibition.
Eyes, lips, fingers
Touching, searching, caressing.
The spiritual becomes consciousness,
Souls entwine as bodies
Recognize one another,
Imagined sensuality, now reality,
Harmony.
HL(M)S 1/28/99

Section III

The Vulnerable Heart

SOLITUDE

As a youth, awkward in adolescence
I surrounded myself with other
Awkward youth, rebelling against
Any and all who stood for the
Establishment, not knowing
Solitude

As a young wife and mother
I filled my life with causes and
People and children still rebelling, but slowly
Becoming the establishment, not knowing
Solitude

As a mature woman, child grown,
Husband gone, I began a search for the
Person I never knew, getting
Acquainted with this woman. I
Became surrounded by the
Solitude

At peace with the woman, loneliness
Seeps into the solitude and once again
I seek community to fill the solitude
To blot out the imperfection of
Age now denying the safety of
Solitude

Cyber Surroundings

Our lives are wrapped in reality
Punctuated by the fantasy
Of moments stolen, creating
The illusion of existence
Pausing once within each hour
Eyes shut tight against surroundings
Breathing in a smile of air
Now walking on Bull Island's beach as
Skylarks swoop up shattering the
Quiet with their laughter
Sharing the picnic at Lady's View
Lost in an ecstasy of surreal touches
Snuggled on the hillside in Forrest Park
Listening to the music of children's voices at play
Standing under the arch gazing at
Tom Sawyer's Mississippi River
With arms wrapped around each other
Savoring the brief time before
Our lives once again become
Wrapped in reality only to be
Punctuated by the fantasy of
Moments stolen in time

Dining Alone

When dining alone you can:
     people watch
     daydream
     organize thoughts
     diet in peace
     memorize
     remember
     frown if you want
     smile to yourself
     pig out
     eat onions
     write
     read
     and cry inside

Life Notes

It seems to me that
A person's life is
Simply a reoccurring melody
Enhanced by the rhythms,
Variations and tempos brought
To you by the lives of others

J. P.

He shapes the music
"Best there is," the kids all say.
Quiet man with dancing eyes.
Heart full of love that only
Spills black dots on a page
In tune with the souls
That surround him. He remains
Alone, to shape the music, that
Entertains the multitude, but,
Only I, will ever know
That the music comes from, the
Quiet man with dancing eyes.

It Happened Again

I can not find order
Within the jumble of
My existence. Time is
But an illusion just
Beyond the reach of memory.
There is no distance,
Only places where those
I love dwell without me.
I can not conceive
Being other than who I am
Yet, I remain trapped in
A constant quest for an
Answer, to a question,
No one has ever asked.

I
Look to the sea
For answers, but
The sea is
Too busy being
The sea.
Her power and
Gentleness hold no
Pretense. She is
Exactly what she is,
The sea, life force
Of a planet.
Rumbling forward
Laying treasures before
Us and quickly
Reclaiming them
Never ceasing
Always at rest,
With purpose and
Destiny, not unlike me,
Her lesson
Simply
Humility. In order
To learn from
Her,
I
Have to allow
Myself to be
Me.

Entanglements

Once our minds entwined
In a thoughtful anticipation of
A time when bliss would be all consuming.
I held the thought of you to my heart and
Cried for a fleeting moment yet to be
In hope our paths would cross again.
2/78

Muddled Mind

You confuse me so with your greatness
My heart longs for you, my mind embraces
Your every thought. You consume me.
Yet, I know you not.
4/86

Preparing for the Journey

Miles melting into miles,
Sunset drifting across the horizon,
Music on the radio,
Sensations tucked into her memory,
Picture on the dashboard,
Fuel for the journey.

Journey

You feel disoriented, then frightened,
Go on a long journey
The end of which, who knows?
You have pain, you're terrified,
Then peace. You tumble down
A long hill, bumping hard on
The way. All reason leaves.
You're ruled by your heart.
It's not horrible, just life and love.

Surreal Surrender

Walking by an azure blue sea,
moon glistening in a starless sky.
Echoes of lonely dreamers looking
for castles, unconquered. Dreams
echoing in the hallways of
tomorrow's light. Windows on
a world of about-to-be.
Waiting for memories rekindled
in her mind. They came together
as figures in a Dali painting.
Their forms melting together
like oils on the canvas.
Captured by the artist in
that moment of bliss.
The surrender, as surreal
as the meeting, never to be
lost, forever captured on the
canvas of her mind.

Colin's Word Picture

Lost in the moment
Gazing into the frame
Deep within the picture
I find myself transported
To a place never visited,
Perceiving smells of food
Cooking in kitchens
Just beyond sight.
Listening with a smile
To the laughter of
Children and lovers over
The horizon, I am there,
For a moment,
Transported from my cares,
Into the word picture.

Forever

I promised you forever and
Gave you only a moment so
Fleeting, yet time enough
To wound you.

I promised you forever, and
In a moment shattered your
Trust and sealed away
Your precious love.

I promised you forever, when
In truth it should have
Only been the moment.

In the blindness of youth I
Saw not my wandering spirit
Only your love.

About To Be

I saw you today
Somehow you looked different,
Was it because we are two no more?
Or is it because you and she are about to be,
Two, I mean, not one and one, but
Two as we once were.
You looked different, kind of vulnerable,
Not perfect as I always saw you,
A little frightened, or cautious I guess.
Questioning your steps, not rushing
As we once did.
Why weren't we friends, then, as we are now?
I still love you even though I try to be angry.
I guess it's only anger at myself
For what was or, could have been,
Yet is no more.

My X

I see beauty in
Dandelions, though you
Call them weeds.
Pretty yellow flowers
To dot my yard
In spring. Leaving
Puffs of wispy
When they're done
For me to blow into the wind
Spreading their cheerful
Color over hill
And yon, yet you
Got weed killer and
Choked my precious
Flowers. I guess
That's why we
Didn't make it and
You're with her and
I'm here alone
With my thoughts.

A Candle on a Shelf

A candle on a shelf
In a quiet room
Flame burned to an ember
Re-ignited by a whispered
Passion blown across
An ocean of salty tears
Cried by unseen lovers
Forgotten in the abyss
The memory of fire returned
At first as lightly as butterfly wings
Then warm and strong like
The wings of eagles soaring high
Above the light of dawn.
Not the raging fire of youth
Simply a strong steady
Curiously mysterious warmth
Not to be analyzed
Only accepted and perhaps
Oh, curious universe perhaps,
Realized.

Saturday Morning

All the poets in heaven conspire
To make me feel their pain.
A lesson of human understanding
Delivered by celestial messengers
Through the cyberspace of reality.
Dreamers dare not hope for
Passions of mortal flesh, only
Glimpses through a
Multi-colored cloudscape
Creating surreal splashes of
What others have and
For she will never be.

Protection

I wrap myself in a blanket
Of silence, shielding my soul
From the cold barbs left
In the wake of passion lost.
Idle chatter serves as balm
On wounds cut into a heart,
Fashioned by lovers during
A kinder time. Gentleness and
Simplicity serve me well and
Time will lift darkness' door.

Capri-Welcome

Oh, bleak room of
  Tables and lost souls
Bawdy lights and dark walls
 A juke box in the corner
Drones out it's melancholy
 Din, a sugar jar, flanked
By salt and pepper, march
 across the table bumping
Only a tin ash tray and
 The lost souls wait for who?

Empty

I reached across space
To touch you, you're not there.
My heart lies open, vulnerable,
I don't even know if you care.
My mind is as restless as
A wind tossed sea,
Awaiting vows of endless love
Pledged from you to me.
But youth and wanderlust
Are on your side, and
I, just someone's forgotten bride.

Saturday Night

There was time to
Remember, but I couldn't.
We danced the two-step and
Sang pretty songs
As a juke-box droned on
Apple-Jack smiled and
The time machine whirred
While you sang about love
The beach stretched east,
Gently, the waves washed west
My mind drifted north
While my body stayed south
Soon the organ grinder
Will find the tune,
The neon will dim and
The pieces will fall in place.

Shallow Moments

We met before the
Band began. We danced and
Sang and laughed and
Then, we waited
For the sun to shine.
The Joker talked
While Lancelot laughed and
The drummer drowned
His pain. Their maidens
Found the wilting rose
Inside their souls. But
Where it ends,
Only heaven knows.

Two Steps Behind

Missing the point
she smiled shyly
always two steps
behind, the music
plays, as fantasies
unfold in aging
minds. Blank eyes
looking back from
nameless faces of
children from the
forgotten time. A mist of tears
clouds our reality
sliding down the mountain
of tomorrow
back to where all
lonesome dreamers go.

Michael

I saw a purple
Moon rising over
Azure blue water
Looking for time
In memories lost
To lovers seen only
In the mist of yesterday's dreams.
Castles built on hopes of
Tomorrow's forgotten moments
Whispered as time
Briefly stops and his
Smile hides the pain
Held deep within his soul
As yesterday passes
Into a Heineken oblivion.

Section IV

A Poetic Heart's Song

Dancing Rhythm

The city street pulses with
A life force only known
To urban dwellers, constant
Back and forth of cars
People and animals on leashes
Music fading in and out
With the waves of movement
Lovers' arms entwined
A lone smiling man with
Glasses and a small brown dog.
Tall, short, black, white, and brown
Speaking language foreign to
The ear, yet contributing
To the music pulsing around the voyeur.
Neon red and blue and yellow
Headlights winking by to where?
Cell phones summoning, urgent voices
From windows above, raindrops
Cause the pace to quicken to a
Dancing rhythm
Thoughts lost and that's how it finishes
Stolen by the street lost in
The pulsing life force.

Crossing The Intercostal

When asked where my words come from
I searched and could only find them
Wrought from the soul of my dream-world
Where I dance with the shadows of
Unasked questions from nameless faces
Brought to my soul on angel wings
shared briefly, written quickly least
They fade into that timeless abyss of
Never more.

Funny

I write bits and pieces,
On bits and pieces,
In hope that one day
an epoch will evolve

Miami Poets

poetry is electricity
floating through the
air landing on the
heart and soul of
wanderers searching for
some kind of meaning
to lives that grow and
expand with the medium of words
poured from lips
as nectar of the gods
given to mortal man

Poetic Musing

Solitude must be good
For me. I write and write
Words spilling out like a
Stream turned into a river mad
With spring rains. Thoughts bumping
Into one another coming faster
Than my pen can write. Verse
Blank, sometimes trite, usually
Poetic, always maddening because
I can't stop it until it's run
It's course and I sit spent, on
A chair, wondering where it
Came from, again!

Mother Sea

As I walk you lay
Your treasures before me.
Bits of coral and broken shell
Torn from your heart,
A rainbow of colors on a
Soft bed of brown, you
Anxiously wash forth to
Reclaim them to the
Safety of your breast.
Your life force simply tears
Of salt. Shed for the men
Who soil your soul
With the byproducts
Of their ignorance.

Miami Drivin'

Went drivin' today
Crossed one of them
Big wide roads
Called a causeway.
Everything in the city's
Got fancy names, you know?
Right there in the
Middle of the hurry
A youngin' an' his Pa
Were fishin'
Memories flooded back
An' I stopped
 "How's it goin" said I?
"Not much," said he.
The youngin' gave me
A toothless grin
"Almost caught me
a big un," he said.
Directly he pulled up
A stringer with a
Healthy minner.
"Really neat," I smiled an
Drove away
Maybe the city's not
So bad after all!

Two Thoughts on the Same Day ☺

I heard today someone say
'There's no such thing as a
dream bigger than your head,
therefore you can not dream big."
But, I smiled and scoffed
For we of big dreams know
The universe, which encompasses
Dreams just simply grows
This is our reality heaven knows.

To find so much beauty
 in one lifetime
  must truly be a gift from God.
  how much sadness I feel
   for those who can not see
    the beauty around them
     for those who only
      find hate and sorrow.
      One must celebrate life
       and all who bring
        joy to it.

View From A Monument/D.C.

Trees marching along
The river bank,
Silent sentries, witness
To a city grown, from
Seeds sown by dreams
From men and women of vision.
Buildings housing the world.
Tributes to those who
Died for a new country
Dedicated to freedom for all.
Words woven into a
Tapestry as alive today as
When they were written.
Life pulsing within her
Concrete as surely as
From the men and women
Who carry her forward
Into the dawn of
A new century.
3/9/91

Spring

Nature awakening from
Her winters rest
Laying a carpet of
Gentle green before
God's creatures to
Soften their rebirth
The cycle of life continues
One born, one dies,
He gives His life so
All might live.
Bare limbs burst
Into an array of color,
Changing each hillside
Into a place of
Reflection, where we
Give thanks for blessings
Pain of daily existence
Is dispelled in the first robin,
Or the cry of a
Newborn calf in search
Of her mother.
Spring is God's way of
Providing us hope.

City rain is:
 gray
 cold
 hard
 bouncing on the concrete
 outside a window

Country rain is:
 clear
 warm
 soft
 soaks into the ground
 all around you.

Spring In chesterfield

they dotted the hillside
awash in new spring grass
two by two
at rest basking in the
warmth of the morning sun
attentive, preening, cooing reassurances to
one another as only lovers can,
i stood alone on the edge
of the hillside
marveling that in spring, even
Canadian geese come in pairs.

Time In A Raindrop

The rain etched patterns
Into the soft plowed earth
While I, snug in the summer kitchen
Watched the flight of a sparrow.
Memories of you on a rain-soaked
Beach, brought a smile.
Eyes shut tight a rainbow danced
Through the salt spray again.
Tears glisten on eyelashes
That play the memory over and over,
Happy moments are only illusions
That disappear when you open your eyes.

Fountain In the Ohio River

Water - shooting upward
From the depths of a
Dark green river, creating
The illusion of a lace
Panel in front of a city,
Busy doing what cities do.
Shop keepers, businessmen,
School boys rushing home
All eager to spend the last
Hours of autumn sunlight.
Children making joyful noises
To be enjoyed, only by moms and
Angels, who listen
For the music in
Their youthful shouts.
A river winding, slowly
Moving to where rivers
Go - soon to join the
Waters of the sea, pulsing
Life force of a blue
Planet, holding secrets
Within her breast
That only dreamers dare
To guess. All tucked
Safely in God's hip pocket.

Just a Breather

I dined alone tonight
  the end of a hectic time.
Weary - a good weary
  reflecting on all that had transpired.
Marching to the timetable set
  by others - not my own.
Puzzling at why, puzzling at why, puzzling at why?

Wishing for a simpler time - wondering
  if there ever was?
Peering into the faces of
  my fellow diners.
Couples, families, others
  who dine alone.
Puzzling at why, puzzling at why, puzzling at why?

Shutting out the cacophony of
  sound, seeking silence.
Yet, surrounding myself with a
  chaos of people.
Desiring anonymity in the
  mass one more nameless face.
Puzzling at why, puzzling at why, puzzling at why?

Unable to bring into focus the images
  drifting by the window.
Seeking, researching, writing
  following the threads left by others.
Always looking in, never out
  such a curious inner universe.
Puzzling at why, puzzling at why, puzzling at why?

Breakfast at the downs

in the early morning hush
five grown women sit
filled with the same awe they felt
as little girls the first time
a thoroughbred glided
as if on wings, past their vision,
across a velvet green pasture.
momentarily forgetting the electric
air of the back track,
Glass separating them from the elements,
each is transported to that
first magical moment when,
these huge powerful beasts became
the symbol for the power each lacked.
language barriers disappeared as a
spiritual understanding emerged.
each knew why, at this moment in time,
they were brought together across continents
to share this unspoken bond of watching
rider and horse, horse and rider
become one with the wind.

Order Form

Postal orders: RiverRock, Inc.
P. O. Box 210205
St. Louis, MO 63121
(314) 610-9999

Please send the following books:

Poetry for Men, by Rock Cottone, $11.95, number of copies ☐

A Journey of the Heart, by H. L. Schnieders, $11.95, number of copies ☐

Name:_____

Address: _____

_____

City: _____ State:_____ Zip:_____

Telephone: (___) _____

Sales tax:
Please add 7.23% for books shipped to Missouri addresses.

Shipping:
$2.50 for the first book and $1.00 for each additional book.

Payment:
☐ Check   ☐ Money Order

Total books:_____ X $11.95 = $_____
Shipping: $_____
Tax: $_____
Total enclosed: $_____